WARRIOR

WORKBOOK 3

Written by:
Floyd Godfrey, LPC, CSAT
Matt Wheeler, LPC, CSAT

Band of Brothers
Workbook 3 - Warrior

Copyright © 2018
Printed by CreateSpace

Title ID: 8455960
ISBN-13: 978-1718916036
ISBN-10: 1718916035

Photography & Graphics: Vecteezy, StockSnap, Texturelib, FreeVector
Graphic Design by Karen Dahlquist / HappyFish

Floyd Godfrey, LPC, CSAT
Matt Wheeler, LPC, CSAT
Family Strategies Counseling Center
www.familystrategies.org
Foundation for Healthy Living (501c3)

1745 S. Alma School Rd. Suite 230
Mesa, AZ 85210
480-668-8301

ACKNOWLEDGEMENTS

These workbooks are the product of working with youth and their parents over the past ten plus years. We are grateful for the ongoing feedback provided to improve and grow the program. Also for the feedback and insight of the adults in our SA program who provided insight to help the youth.

This program would not be here today if it weren't for our Contributing Editors Jan Gibbons and Jeni Linn.

Thank you.

WARRIOR

WORKBOOK 3

CONTENTS

WARRIOR RANK

We use a ranking system to help all participants in the program move through each step required to achieve long-term success. We've established "ranks," or different "levels" of achievement. The more work you put into recovery, the further up your rank you climb. It's up to you. There are five ranks to-

tal. Graduation means that you've completed the tasks of every rank, and become a "Commander."

Good recovery means more than simply NOT slipping. It means making changes inside you.

Each rank contains eight areas of focus. These "pillars" help you grow. You will complete a required task for each pillar in every rank. Lessons in the workbooks are educational and not the sole purpose of the program. It you want good recovery, strive to make changes within yourself.

8 — EMOTIONAL AWARENESS

7 — FAMILY SYSTEMS

6 — SELF-ESTEEM

5 — SOBRIETY SKILL IMPROVMENT

4 — SOCIAL SKILL DEVELOPMENT

3 — EDUCATION (RELATED TO RECOVERY)

2 — SHAME REDUCTION

1 — SUPPORT NETWORK DEVELOPMENT

It might be important for you to know, that when counselors help young men overcome sexual compulsivity, these "pillars" are the same areas of focus they write into their official treatment plans. Although counselors may vary a bit, achieving solid success occurs when using these eight essential pillars.

1. *Support Network Development*
2. *Shame Reduction*
3. *Recovery Education*
4. *Social Skill Development*
5. *Sobriety Skill Improvement*
6. *Self-Esteem Development*
7. *Family System Cultivation*
8. *Emotional Awareness*

As you work through the "ranks," make sure and have your therapist date and initial when you complete a task. On some items your parents can sign. You'll need to complete this workbook before moving on to the next. We wrote these workbooks with lessons and tasks specifically designed to go hand-in-hand with the eight "Ranking Pillars" to assist you in your successful recovery. Be patient with yourself, as it takes time to grow and learn the skills necessary for solid recovery.

Congratulations on joining a brotherhood that wants to support you. Strength comes from unity. Ask questions and reach out for help when you need. We work together as a team. Good luck!

RANK 3: WARRIOR

TARGET DATE: _____

1. With the help of a group leader, identify another group member who may need some mentorship in his life. Discuss with him your goal to learn mentoring, and ask him what you could do to support him. Do something two (or more) times a week that would be mentoring, over a four week period.

DATE: _____ INITIAL: _____

DATE: _____ INITIAL: _____

DATE: _____ INITIAL: _____

DATE: _____ INITIAL: _____

2. Call someone from group every day for one week and check on them to see how they're doing. Ask them specifically about school, family, and recovery challenges. (This is about you supporting someone else). This should be someone different than in task "a" above.

DATE: _____ INITIAL: _____

3. Complete a sexual history and discuss with your therapist during individual counseling.

DATE: _____ INITIAL: _____

4. Complete **Lesson Nine** and discuss with your therapist during individual counseling.

DATE: _____ INITIAL: _____

5. Complete **Lesson Ten** and discuss with your therapist during individual counseling.

DATE: _____ INITIAL: _____

6. Complete **Lesson Eleven** and discuss with your therapist during individual counseling.

DATE: _____ INITIAL: _____

7. Complete **Lesson Twelve** and discuss with your therapist during individual counseling.

DATE: _____ INITIAL: _____

8. With your therapist, identify a specific way to increase your social interaction. Follow through on the activity and discuss during individual counseling.

DATE: _____ INITIAL: _____

9. Complete the "Wardawg" challenge.

DATE: _____ INITIAL: _____

10. Identify 3 anonymous "acts of service" you can do for family members and do them secretly. Report these acts to the group.

DATE: _____ INITIAL: _____

11. With your therapist, identify an incident that has happened which was emotionally upsetting to you. Process the event during group time.

DATE: _____ INITIAL: _____

12. Perform a "grit" exercise during group.

DATE: _____ INITIAL: _____

13. Write a page about how a positive self-esteem helps a young man in recovery, and then discuss your writing with your therapist.

DATE: _____ INITIAL: _____

GOAL CHART

DATE:

GOALS	SUN	MON	TUES	WED	THURS	FRI	SAT
Example: *Finish Lesson Nine*	X	X	X	X			
Example: *Call my mentor*		X		X			X
Example: *Write in my journal*			X			X	

DATE:

GOALS	SUN	MON	TUES	WED	THURS	FRI	SAT

DATE:

GOALS	SUN	MON	TUES	WED	THURS	FRI	SAT

GOAL CHART

DATE:

GOALS	SUN	MON	TUES	WED	THURS	FRI	SAT

DATE:

GOALS	SUN	MON	TUES	WED	THURS	FRI	SAT

DATE:

GOALS	SUN	MON	TUES	WED	THURS	FRI	SAT

GOAL CHART

DATE:

GOALS	SUN	MON	TUES	WED	THURS	FRI	SAT

DATE:

GOALS	SUN	MON	TUES	WED	THURS	FRI	SAT

DATE:

GOALS	SUN	MON	TUES	WED	THURS	FRI	SAT

GOAL CHART

DATE:

GOALS	SUN	MON	TUES	WED	THURS	FRI	SAT

DATE:

GOALS	SUN	MON	TUES	WED	THURS	FRI	SAT

DATE:

GOALS	SUN	MON	TUES	WED	THURS	FRI	SAT

GOAL CHART

DATE:

GOALS	SUN	MON	TUES	WED	THURS	FRI	SAT

DATE:

GOALS	SUN	MON	TUES	WED	THURS	FRI	SAT

DATE:

GOALS	SUN	MON	TUES	WED	THURS	FRI	SAT

GOAL CHART

DATE:

GOALS	SUN	MON	TUES	WED	THURS	FRI	SAT

DATE:

GOALS	SUN	MON	TUES	WED	THURS	FRI	SAT

DATE:

GOALS	SUN	MON	TUES	WED	THURS	FRI	SAT

WAR PLAN

WAR PLAN

My Bottom Lines:

_____

_____

_____

My First Aid Kit (and/or Travel Kit):

I will complete my kit by: _____

Reach out tool: _____

_____

Meetings:

Individual counseling sessions: _____

_____

_____

12-Step or other support group meetings: _____

_____

_____

Personal Reflection:

Read (_at least 15 minutes recovery reading daily_): _____

_____

_____

Journal: _____

_____

_____

Spirituality:

Prayer or meditation: _____

_____

_____

Scriptural or religious reading: _____

_____

_____

Service to others: _____

_____

_____

Exercise:

At least 30 minutes daily: _____

_____

_____

Rest and Relaxation Guidelines:

Get adequate sleep: _____

_____

_____

Take healthy breaks: _____

_____

_____

Little or no TV: _____

_____

_____

Social Media: _____

_____

_____

Nutritional Guidelines:

Eat three balanced meals a day: _____

_____

_____

Healthy snacks between meals: _____

Avoid getting hungry: _____

_____

Avoid junk food: _____

_____

Other Interests:

Music: _____

_____

Reading: _____

_____

Find something healthy that you enjoy doing: _____

_____

Develop your talents: _____

_____

Additional Notes:

_____

_____

_____

_____

_____

_____

_____

_____

BAND OF BROTHERS

LESSON 9: TEAM SUPPORT

TEAM SUPPORT

As we discussed previously, "isolation" is one of the biggest roadblocks faced by teens in recovery. For long-term success you need to develop "Team Support." It's important that you've found a group like Band of Brothers—a place to share your concerns, struggles and secrets. You also need adults, mentors and friends with whom you can share. When you have these pieces in place, then you have support. Recovery is a team sport!

Young men are often afraid to open up and develop team support. They might think, "Why would anyone want to know about my type of problem?" Or, "No one else has issues this embarrassing." Sometimes a teen wants to do everything on his own. Perhaps it may have been emotionally unsafe to reach out in the past. Have you ever watched people get teased when they try to share something personal? If so, you understand why some young men will hesitate to reach out.

As you develop team support, you must determine who is mature and safe. This kind of safety looks different. For example, some teens need:

- *Assurance the person will keep it private, without gossip.*
- *Assurance the person will not be judgmental.*
- *Assurance the person will keep it off social media.*

1. Think of what creates safety for you. List as many items as you can think of that help you feel safe with others:

no judgment, confidentiality, I need encouragement,
overall safety

_____

_____

_____

_____

_____

2. Now think of the other teenagers in your therapy group. What do YOU need to do for THEM to be safe with you? In other words… how will you show safety for THEM:

_____ No judgement! _____

_____ Keep it confidential _____

_____ Be there for them. _____

_____

_____

_____

In Band of Brothers each member needs to develop safe communication with others. There will be times you NEED to talk to someone your own age for support. This would be in addition to your mentor or the trusted adults in your life.

Remember that you should be calling and connecting with others even when you are in a good place. In other words, you understand that continuing to connect with support is critical—regardless of whether you're having a hard time, or sailing through life without challenges.

When someone calls YOU for support, there are good ways you can help. The chart below describes five important aspects of empathy. When you learn how to use any of the five points below, you'll be able to provide good support.

EMPATHY FOR SUPPORT

Perspective	Consider the perspective of the other person. Can you relate to how they feel and why they feel this way?
No Judgments	Stay out of judgments. Don't assume you have the answer they need. Don't try to fix it. Make sure your own emotions don't get in the way.
Feelings	Recognize what they are feeling. Are they feeling sad? Angry? Afraid? Embarrassed? Hurt? Joy?
Emotions	Mirror their emotion as you feel it. This helps them to understand that you are in this with them. Try and relate to the emotion they are going through.
Ask	Tell them how you feel about them sharing. Such as, "I am glad you trust me enough to share with me." Make sure to ask the person if there's anything that you can do to support them beyond listening.

On the following pages you will see examples of language that people use when they're showing empathy using the previous 5 aspects.

PERSPECTIVE TAKING

- *If that happened to me I'd feel…*
- *When that happened to me I felt…*
- *I think I can understand why you feel that way. I think I would feel that too if…*
- *I can't imagine what that would be like, but I think I've felt similar when this happened to me…*
- *I don't blame you for feeling that way … I can see why you feel… You have every right to feel… I would feel similar (or) I feel that too as you are sharing with me right now.*
- *I am so glad you are letting me listen because this would make me feel…*

3. Suppose a guy from group calls and tells you he's really depressed because he's failing a class. Write below a response that would be "perspective taking:"

I'm sorry to hear that man… I've had some tough classes too this year and I too felt angry at depressed at myself for not being good enough, so I know that feeling all too well…

STAY OUT OF JUDGEMENT

AVOID Language such as:

- *You should…*
- *I know what you need…*
- *I told you before that…*
- *Why don't you…*
- *How come you did that…*
- *If you would just…*

- *You told me that…*
- *You said you weren't…*

When seeking more information, you might try…

- *I can tell that this is upsetting, scary, exciting etc. … but I want to make sure I understand… (restate what you have heard and allow the person to elaborate more)… so this happened? Then you went over there?*

- *Is there anything more you want to share because I want to make sure I understand…*

- *Thank you for sharing I am so glad you told me.*

4. Suppose a guy from group calls and tells you he's really depressed because his parents have grounded him. Write below a response that would be "Stay Out of Judgment:"

> I told you not to do that because
> it would make your
> parents angry.
> now you know why!

REMEMBER – *anything that sounds like a "Fix it" or a judgment in anyway jeopardizes your ability to connect with the person. Don't ever try and fix. Ever. You can ask if they are open to feedback or if they want some advice, but be careful.*

RECOGNIZE THE EMOTION

Warning for this part of the empathy step, the language only happens in your head! Don't say this out loud:

Avoid language in your head like:

- *What are they going on about now?*
- *They are so ridiculous?*
- *How many times have they gone on about this same old garbage?*
- *They have no right to be sad, angry, mad etc. I am the one that should be…*

Ask yourself questions like this:

- *I can tell they are feeling some emotion… what does it look like they are feeling?*
- *What emotion are they feeling? Is it closest to sadness, anger, fear, shame, etc.?*

4. Suppose a brother from the group calls and tells you he's really nervous because he's failing a class and his parents don't know. Write below a response that would be "Recognize the Emotion:"

"I think he must be scared if he told me he's nervous. His parents are probably strict with grades and he's embarassed to tell them… shame might come with it if his parents find out.

COMMUNICATE THAT EMOTION TO OTHERS

- *It seems like you are feeling... is that right?*
- *If I am understanding correctly you are feeling...*
- *I am so sorry you are feeling... I am glad you are telling me and I want to support you.*
- *I am so glad you are letting me know you feel...*
- *Thank you for trusting me enough to share your feelings with me.*
- *I don't even know what to say, I'm just so glad you told me.*

When you first begin, it may feel robotic and disingenuous. But the only way to learn is to practice. Use these tools and don't be afraid to admit that in the past you could have done better. Remember that it takes practice to give good support. Don't give up! Practice these skills in all your interactions with others.

Did you notice that nowhere in showing empathy did you ever try and fix it?

_____Yes._____

_____

_____

6. Suppose a guy from the group calls and tells you he's really excited because a girl he likes accepted his invitation to Prom. Write below a response that would be "Communicate that Emotion to Others:"

___That's awesome man! I can tell you are____

___pretty happy! How did it go???___

_____

_____

_____

_____

_____

_____

ASK WHAT YOU CAN DO

Expressing support is a very simple but important interaction in building friendships and it does NOT require you to have answers or solutions. You simply ask a question. Don't try to solve anything for them. Just ask. Be present. Walk with them. This might feel like doing nothing and that's okay. But you are doing what they need by just being available. Here are common ways of expressing support:

- *Is there anything that I can do to support you?*
- *How can I help you?*
- *Is there something you need from me?*
- *How can I be there for you?*
- *What would be the best way for me to support you right now?*
- *How can I support you?*
- *I am so glad you shared with me. It reminds me how much trust we share.*
- *I am glad you feel safe to tell me these things.*
- *When you share with me, it reminds me that I can share whatever I need to with you.*
- *You are brave for opening up. Have you told anyone else?*

7. Suppose a brother from the group calls and tells you he's really discouraged because he just slipped in his recovery. Write below a response that would be "Ask What You Can Do:"

Thanks for letting me know, that takes a lot of courage to trust me, so thank you, I wanna let you know that I'm here for you man! what do you need from me so next time we can avoid this?

Practice using the different styles of supporting through empathy with your therapist in a session. Ask to share a frustrating experience you had with a friend or something that made them feel sad or embarrassed. The scenario could be something you experienced in the past or something fictional your therapist creates. The idea is to practice your words and responses. Since empathy is a skill, it can be practiced and developed just like throwing a football. The more you practice, the better you become. The great thing about the skill of empathy is that you can use it in every relationship you have for the rest of your life.

8. What was most difficult when practicing with your therapist?

_____

_____

_____

_____

_____

_____

_____

_____

9. During your group therapy, ask for time to practice empathy. Role play a situation that someone may have experienced and use empathy. What did you do well when practicing with your group?

_____

_____

_____

_____

_____

_____

_____

_____

LESSON 10: THE DRAMA TRIANGLE

THE DRAMA TRIANGLE

Have you heard of the Bermuda triangle where ships get lost and planes crash? Mystery abounds in this strange place of the world. People who study behavior have discovered a frightening and more dangerous triangle. One that affects your personal life. It's called the DRAMA triangle. It's a crazy cycle of interaction we all find ourselves in at times with the people around us! The drama triangle illustrates how you might interact with family members, teachers, church leaders, girls, or with buddies. It could involve anyone. This triangle ruins relationships. It causes hurt feelings. It causes anger and frustration. Life becomes an emotional blender if you live in the drama triangle. Healthy relationships cannot function in the triangle. The triangle involves three roles: Victim, Persecutor, and Rescuer. Which role do you fall into with people? You might find that you take on one role really well. Or you might find that all of them fit you from time to time depending on with whom you are interacting.

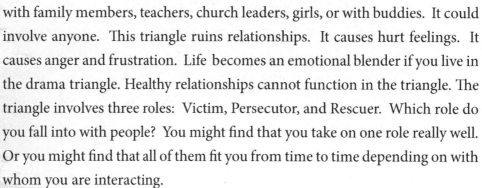

Look at the list on the following pages and place a check mark on any role with which you identify to determine which roles are <u>most</u> applicable to you. Then total your marks at the end. It's not bad if you identify with any of these statements. It's important that you be honest with yourself and become aware

of the emotional craziness in the midst of the drama triangle. Once you can see you're in the triangle, it'll be easier to escape.

Life is better outside the triangle!

VICTIM

Victims feel sorry for themselves. They often feel everyone picks on them. They think they aren't good enough. Victims often feel powerless or incapable. They might feel defective or broken.

1. Go down this list and mark any of the items that you think you do:

☒ I have **more problems** than most of my friends.

☐ I'm **not worthy** of having good friends.

☐ When people try to help me, I think of **reasons why it won't work**.

☐ **I hold in my anger** until I feel ready to explode.

☐ I feel **sorry** for myself.

☐ **I resent** others' success and popularity.

☐ **I blame others** in my thoughts, but I don't voice it.

☒ **No one understands** me or I feel always misunderstood

☐ **I play dumb** when I am confronted about a problem.

☐ I find it difficult to **speak up** for **myself.**

☐ I often **whine and complain**.

☒ I often feel like I am always **in trouble**.

☐ I constantly tell myself that I'm **"not doing it right."**

Victim Total: _3_

RESCUER

Rescuers identify themselves as fixers and help-ers. They believe in the goodness of helping and see themselves as essential to help others. Res-cuers often don't let others solve their own chal-lenges. They're always stepping in to fix it. The problem is, these actions of helping often "dis-able" others. A rescuer will help another person, even when that person can do it without help.

2. Go down this list and mark any of the items that you think you do:

☐ I try to **help** people even when they tell me they **don't want my help**.

☒ I feel **compelled to help** others with their problems.

☒ I feel **guilty** if I **don't take care** of my friends' problems.

☐ I get **offended** if people don't realize **how much I've done for them**.

☒ I find myself **in the middle** of friends who are fighting.

☒ I feel **bad about saying "no"** and always volunteer for things.

☒ I take on the **burdens and worries of friends**.

☒ I put everyone else's **feelings before my own**.

☒ I help others **keep secrets**.

☐ I feel that **I'm better** than most of my friends and family.

☒ I focus on others to **avoid focusing on myself**.

Rescuer Total: __8__

PERSECUTOR

Persecutors ignore that they have weaknesses. They focus on the weaknesses or problems of others. They attempt to avoid uncomfortable feelings inside themselves by making offensive, sarcastic, or blunt remarks. They often spend time around people whom they can criticize or tease. Persecutors use power over others by lecturing, preaching, criticizing, or teasing. Some persecutors are known for their bad tempers, or for being sarcastic, defensive, pushy, controlling or rude. Sometimes people are afraid to say anything to them.

3. Go down this list and mark any of the items that you think you do:

- ☐ **I blame everyone else** for problems.
- ☒ I have to be in **control** of the conversation.
- ☒ I often find myself **preaching or giving advice** to others.
- ☐ **I lecture** my friends, parents, siblings, and others about their problems.
- ☐ **I verbally attack** others – I'm rude.
- ☐ **I interrogate** my parents or friends.
- ☐ **I bully or tease** siblings or others around me.
- ☐ I make **sarcastic remarks**.
- ☐ I am **critical** of those around me.
- ☐ I often make **cutting remarks** and am known for being **"blunt."**
- ☐ I attempt to **control** my friends or siblings.

Persecutor Total: 2

Now go back and look at your totals.

	VICTIM
	RESCUER
	PERSECUTOR

4. Which category has the most marks? _Rescuer_

Once you identify which trait is most common for you, you'll see where most of the craziness comes from. You can then learn how to escape the drama and step out of the triangle—whether with a friend, a girl, your parents, a pastor, a youth leader or a teacher. Perhaps the drama is with yourself inside your own head. Wherever the triangle, the goal is to get out!

An escape route from the triangle looks like this:

- *Acknowledge it's happening - tell someone what corner of the triangle you're in.*

- *Ask yourself, "Why am I behaving this way?" Be honest.*

- *Don't become emotional and write down logical actions.*

- *Do the logical thing. Take action right now to step out of the triangle.*

EXAMPLE ONE

Blake is angry. He took a girl he was crushing on to Senior Prom. Half way through the night she disappeared with another boy. She bailed on him. Blake began arguing in his own head with the other boy. Although nobody knew it, he was cursing and screaming at the boy for what he did. Soon he recognized that he was really emotional and that he was clenching his fists. He felt like throwing up. He hated the way he was feeling. Then he realized he was in the drama triangle and making everything worse for himself. He left the dance and when he got home, he took out a pad of paper and wrote down his escape route:

1. I can see that I'm in the drama triangle. I'm super upset and it's making a bad situation worse. I'm going to go tell Jackson from group what happened. I'm in the persecutor corner. I'm wanna break something!

2. I'm actually not sure if I'm as much angry as I am sad. Geesh. Now I feel like crying. I'm super depressed! How could she dump me like that? I'm really embarrassed. Will the other guys laugh at me? OMG, it feels like I will never get past this. I'm super down and depressed. This is overwhelming.

3. It's hard not be emotional, but I can talk to the guys in group about this. I can also share more with Jackson - he'll understand. I think I just need to talk to some people about this horrible experience. At least I don't have to be alone or fall into the victim corner.

4. I'm getting up right now and going to go ask Jackson to come to the hallway so I can tell him. I hope I don't cry.

EXAMPLE TWO

Ethan is super embarrassed. He was having a bad day. Nothing went right at school. Some of the guys were picking on him in PE. Then a girl in one of his classes made fun of him. When he finally got home, he went straight to his bedroom so he could look at porn. He didn't even care about trying to stay sober. He plopped down at his desk, opened his cell phone and within a few minutes found some images. Then suddenly his mother was behind him asking for his phone. She had seen everything he was doing. He handed her the phone and started talking to himself… "I'm such a loser. Nothing ever works out for me. Why is my life such a disaster? My mom will never trust me again." Then he realized he was in the drama triangle and making everything worse. So he got out a pad of paper and wrote down his escape route:

1. I can see that I'm in the drama triangle. I'm super upset and it's making a bad situation worse. I'm going to go tell Jace from group what happened and that I'm in the victim corner. I just feel like crap!

2. I know I'm feeling sorry for myself because I'm so humiliated. Everyone's been picking on me today. I was already having a bad day. I just need to feel appreciated by someone.

3. I can share with some other guys from group about what happened. I can go talk to my mom and tell her I'm embarrassed. I could write a plan to fix this with my parents.

4. I'm going to call the guys in group right now (or talk to the guys in group tonight) about all this.

Now it's your turn. Think of two different times you were in a drama triangle. Write briefly about each occurrence, and then share it with your therapist in session. Have your therapist help you fill in the "escape route" section of each example. Your therapist should review your answers with you.

5. Situation One - Inside the Triangle

I was in the drama triangle when…

it felt like the world was against me. nothing feels as if it's going my way and I'm really angry at myself because I feel like the burden. It feels as if I'm in the victim corner.

6. Situation One - Escape Route

A. Acknowledge that it's happening - tell someone what corner you're in. Write this step below for your situation.

_____
_____
_____
_____

B. Ask yourself why you are behaving this way - be honest. Now write your honest answer below.

_____
_____
_____
_____
_____
_____

C. Don't become emotional and write down logical actions. Write down the action you could take to get out of the triangle.

_____
_____
_____
_____
_____

D. Do the logical thing. Take action right now to get out of the triangle. Write down what you are going to do, or did do, to actually get out of the triangle.

_____
_____
_____
_____
_____
_____

7. Situation Two - Inside the Triangle

I was in the drama triangle when…

I noticed I'd rather care for others, but not give myself the same treatment. I wanna help everyone else right now to cover up my own emotions to make me feel better. I'm trying to be the Rescuer.

8. Situation Two - Escape Route

A. Acknowledge that it's happening - tell someone what corner you're in. Write this step below for your situation.

B. Ask yourself why you are behaving this way - be honest. Now write your honest answer below.

_____

_____

_____

_____

_____

C. Don't become emotional and write down logical actions. Write down the action you could take to get out of the triangle.

_____

_____

_____

_____

_____

_____

D. Do the logical thing. Take action right now to get out of the triangle. Write down what you are going to do, or did do, to actually get out of the triangle.

_____

_____

_____

_____

_____

Do you want to live outside the triangle?

It might sound weird, but it's common to get into your own drama triangle in your own mind. See if you can predict future triangles that might occur. This will help you prepare to avoid them or get out of them more quickly.

9. Write down a possible drama triangle that might occur in the future.

_____ - Prom _____

_____ - Drama _____

_____ - Relationships _____

10. What role might you fall into?

_____ - Prom - victim _____
_____ - Drama - rescuer _____
_____ - Relationships - rescuer, _____

11. Who were you in the triangle with?

_____ — _____

12. Did you get into any triangles in your own mind?

13. What is the escape route you might use for this triangle?

NOTES

_____
_____
_____
_____
_____
_____
_____
_____
_____
_____
_____
_____
_____
_____
_____
_____
_____
_____
_____
_____
_____
_____
_____
_____
_____
_____
_____
_____
_____

LESSON 11: GRIT

THE PARABLE OF THE EAGLE

By James Aggrey

(http://holyjoe.org/poetry/anon3.htm)

Once upon a time, while walking through the forest, a certain man found a young eagle. He took it home and put it in his barnyard where it soon learned to eat chicken feed and to behave as chickens behave.

One day, a naturalist who was passing by inquired of the owner why it was that an eagle, the king of all birds, should be confined to live in the barnyard with the chickens. "Since I have given it chicken feed and trained it to be a chicken, it has never learned to fly," replied the owner. "It behaves as chickens behave, so it is no longer an eagle."

"Still," insisted the naturalist, "it has the heart of an eagle and can surely be taught to fly."

It takes grit to be an eagle.

After talking it over, the two men agreed to find out whether this was possible. Gently, the naturalist took the eagle in his arms and said, "You belong to the sky and not to the earth. Stretch forth your wings and fly."

The eagle, however, was confused; he did not know who he was, and seeing the chickens eating their feed, he jumped down to be with them again.

Un-detoured, the next day the naturalist took the eagle up on the roof of the house and urged him again. "You are an eagle. Stretch forth your wings and fly." But the eagle was afraid of his unknown self and world and jumped down once more for the chicken feed.

On the third day, the naturalist rose early and took the eagle out of the barnyard to a high mountain. There, he held the king of birds high above him and encouraged him again, saying, "You are an eagle. You belong to the sky as well as the earth. Stretch forth your wings now, and fly."

The eagle looked around, back toward the barnyard and up to the sky. Still he did not fly. Then the naturalist lifted him straight toward the sun and it happened that the eagle began to tremble and slowly he stretched his wings. At last, with a triumphant cry, he soared away into the heavens.

It may be that the eagle still remembers the chickens with nostalgia; it may even be that he occasionally revisits the barnyard. But as far as anyone knows, he has never returned to lead the life of a chicken. He was an eagle even though he had been kept and tamed as a chicken. Just like the eagle, people who have learned to think of themselves as something they aren't can re-decide in favor of their real potential. They can become "eagles" and soar.

INTELLIGENCE & GRIT

Intelligence is the ability to learn and Grit is the ability to endure. The difference between the two is important. You can learn many things about recovery, but you must have endurance to succeed. Recovery requires perseverance and passion for your long-term goal. You could be really smart, but not have any motivation. You might have good grades at school, but never accomplish anything in your life.

1.What does it mean to be intelligent?

_____

_____

_____

_____

_____

2. In your own words, what is "grit"?

_____

_____

_____

_____

_____

3. In what areas of your life do you already display a lot of grit?

_____

_____

_____

_____

4. How could someone be intelligent in recovery but lack grit?

_____

_____

_____

_____

5. In what aspects of your life do you lack grit?

_____

_____

_____

_____

6. Why would grit be important in your recovery?

_____

_____

_____

_____

_____

7. What are some ways for you to develop grit in your recovery?

_____

_____

_____

_____

_____

Vision for Life

Young men face decisions such as considering whether or not to go to college, and if so, which one? They seek to determine which professional career they will enjoy and is best suited to them. These decisions impact the rest of their lives. Standards and morals become increasingly important. Setting goals and creating a vision for your life becomes a key component to growing up. Not having goals and a lack of vision results in stagnancy, confusion and frustration.

Similarly, you must have a vision for your recovery. What are the specific reasons you are trying to clean up your life? Why do you want to get sober? What are your motivations for getting better? Sometimes the reasons for recovery are weak. Look at the following examples:

- *John came to his counselor because his parents forced him.*
- *Larry isn't acting out because he wants people to stop talking about it.*
- *Paul decided to join Band of Brothers because everybody thought he should.*
- *Jason got into Band of Brothers because he can't participate in certain church duties.*
- *Pete is trying to stop looking at X-rated websites because his girlfriend is really mad about his pornography use.*

8. The reasons above will be INSUFFICIENT to carry a young man through a successful recovery. Can you think of the reasons why? List the reasons below.

_____

_____

_____

_____

_____

9. What were some of the weaker reasons why you might have started recovery?

_____

_____

_____

_____

_____

10. Consider the REAL reasons you want to be in recovery. What are the compelling reasons that would keep you working on your issues long-term? Try and think deeper about it. Write your "vision" for recovery below. What does it look like? What are the reasons you're doing this?

_____

_____

_____

_____

11. To complete this lesson, participate in a grit exercise during group time. Write below what the experience was like. What did you learn from it?

_____

_____

_____

_____

_____

_____

"Fall seven times,
stand up eight."

-Japanese Proverb

THE STORY OF TERRY FOX

www.terryfox.org

Terry Fox was born in Winnipeg, Manitoba. As a toddler he stacked wooden blocks tirelessly. If they tumbled down, he'd try again and again until they stayed in place. Terry developed patience and as a child he loved games that lasted a long time. He could amuse himself for hours. Sometimes he set up a table-hockey game and devised a long, complicated season's schedule. He would play for both teams, allowing three passes before he would switch sides and shoot for the other team. Terry also loved playing with toy soldiers. He would bundle up carpets and make fortresses in the basement, arranging his armies of cowboys and Indians or soldiers from both world wars on either side. When the soldiers lay face down, they were dead; face up, they were wounded. He fought to the last man.

In elementary school, he played baseball. Sometimes he'd arrive an hour early at the corner where he was to pick up his ride, just to make sure he'd get to the park on time. When they were in eighth grade, the PE teacher in Junior High School, noticed Terry. Terry was "the little guy who worked his rear off. If there was a race, he'd be in the middle of the pack."

In eleventh grade, Terry joined the High School basketball team. His father remembered Terry once scored twenty points in the first half of a game. "He'd become somebody by working hard," his father said. Even when the team was being clobbered, the basketball coach, recalled that Terry never gave up.

Later that year, Terry joined the cross-country team. He worked hard and soon became an accomplished runner. He competed the British Columbia cross-country finals taking second place. Terry received 'Athlete of the Year' award in twelfth grade.

> "The running I can do, even if I have to crawl every last mile."
> -Terry Fox

All his life success quickly turned when Terry was 19. Doctors discovered that he had cancer. The disease would steal his leg, by forcing an amputation six inches above the knee. He recalls: "The night before my amputation, my former basketball coach brought me a magazine with an article on an amputee who ran in the New York Marathon. It was then I decided to meet this new challenge head on and not only overcome my disability, but conquer it in such a way that I could never look back and say it disabled me. But I soon realized that that would only be half my quest, for as I went through the 16 months of the physically and emotionally draining ordeal of chemotherapy, I was rudely awakened by the feelings that surrounded and coursed through the cancer clinic. There were faces with the brave smiles, and the ones who had given up smiling. There were feelings of hopeful denial, and the feelings of despair.

"Somewhere the hurting must stop..."

TERRY FOX
1958 - 1981

From the beginning the going was extremely difficult, and I was facing chronic ailments foreign to runners with two legs in addition to the common physical strains felt by all dedicated athletes.

But these problems are now behind me, as I have either out-persisted or learned to deal with them. I feel strong not only physically, but more important, emotionally. Soon I will be adding one full mile a week, and coupled with weight training I have been doing, by next April I will be ready to achieve something that for me was once only a distant dream reserved for the world of miracles.

The running I can do, even if I have to crawl every last mile.

_____

"I am not a dreamer, and I am not saying that this will initiate any kind of definitive answer or cure to cancer. But I believe in miracles. I have to."

LESSON 12: SEXUALIZED EMOTIONS

SEXUALIZED EMOTIONAL ENERGY

It's really important to know that emotional energy can sometimes influence your sexual fantasies or attractions. Natural sexual urges have a sort of "magnetism" that draws them toward emotional energy. The stronger the emotional energy, the stronger the draw on your sexuality. By analyzing your sexual fantasies and attractions, you can discover underlying emotions needs or wounds. When you resolve the emotions underneath, temptation will often decrease. It can help make easier to manage your sexual urges, and decrease the obsession.

Sometimes strong emotions emerge from wounds or unmet needs for attachment. Boys who are abused emotionally, physically or sexually have been wounded. Other traumatic experiences with family or peers can be upsetting and cause emotional hurt or pain. High School experiences with teachers and coaches can be wounding as well.

Emotions are the force that drives us and steers our mind in different directions.

Have you ever been sexually obsessed to the point you didn't feel in control? The obsessive nature of your sexual urges could reflect powerful emotions or wounds which are unresolved.

It's easier to stay sober when sexual urges aren't so obsessive. Resolving wounds and decreasing intense emotional energy becomes important. However, this doesn't mean that you will stop having sexual feelings. Your sexuality will always be part of you. But if you're doing good recovery work, your sexual feelings won't rule your life obsessively.

Healthy sexuality involves an innocent curiosity and desire for closeness, not an obsessive drive that overpowers your day and takes over your life.

1. *Fill in the blanks:*

- It's really important to know that your _____ influence your _____ feelings.

- The stronger the _____ the stronger the influence on your _____ will be.

- When you resolve the emotions or wounds underneath, your _____ often diminish.

- Sometimes these emotions are strong because they come from_____.

You might be wondering what type of "emotion" could become sexualized? If the feelings are intense, almost any emotion can weave into your sexual drive. The list could include any emotional wounds or traumas. It could also include your natural need for attachment (or the lack of attachment). Sexualizing emotions could include memories or experiences from earlier in life. Your sexual drive can weave into any feeling. Although it doesn't necessarily happen to everyone, identifying any emotional undercurrent will help you in recovery.

ANALYZE THE EMOTIONAL ENERGY

Now see if you can analyze some examples of what we're talking about. Read each example and circle the possible outcome. Remember, you are looking for "emotional energy" underneath sexual urges. Discuss each example with your therapist during a counseling session.

EXAMPLE ONE - Mason

Mason was bullied as a child and constantly picked on by older kids. The experience took away his sense of control. He never told anyone and simply became an angry person. His parents took away his computer and restricted his activities. They gave him very strict rules. Mason became increasingly angry and started to crave a sense of control in his life. He started doing "controlling" behaviors with his friends. He got a bit pushy and manipulative. Eventually this starting showing up in his sexual feelings. He had thoughts about sexually manipulating others, and fantasies about doing aggressive sexual activity.

2. One day he realized, "I'm sexualizing my _____."

3. Discuss with your therapist any emotions or feelings that Mason could be sexualizing. Consider these possible examples: a need to control, desire to manipulate, frustration or rage.

_____

_____

_____

_____

_____

4. Discuss with your therapist what the possible triggers might be for these examples.

_____

_____

_____

_____

_____

EXAMPLE TWO - Cody

Cody struggled with anxiety. He was always nervous and shy. At school he rarely talked to girls. He only spoke to kids at school when they spoke to him first. He was constantly wishing that someone would notice him. He wanted someone to reach out and see who he was on the inside. He desperately wanted a girl to care about his private world. Cody also has seven siblings and continually felt unseen by his parents. He felt invisible sitting at the dinner table each night - no one talked to him. Eventually this starting showing up in his sexual feelings. He had thoughts about exposing himself naked in public. He started to fantasize about showing his private parts to girls in his class. He was even tempted to unzip his pants when he was alone after school with a teacher.

5. One day he realized, "I'm sexualizing my _____."

6. Discuss with your therapist any emotions or feelings that Cody could be sexualizing. Consider these possible examples: desire to be noticed by parents and friends, need to feel important to someone, desire to be seen for who he is inside.

_____

_____

_____

_____

_____

_____

7. Discuss with your therapist what the possible triggers might be for these examples.

_____

_____

_____

_____

_____

EXAMPLE THREE - Kyle

Kyle started puberty a little later than the other boys. When his buddies were discussing body changes and girls, he found himself not understanding what they were talking about. His curiosity intensified about everything sexual - girl's bodies, boy's bodies, intercourse, masturbation, and pornography. As he started growing more, he found his mind filled with images of naked people and sexual behavior. He wanted to try things he hadn't done before and experience the excitement of adult sexual activity. Eventually this starting showing up in his sexual feelings. He had thoughts about doing sexual things with his peers. Even his dreams at night became filled with sexual imagery.

8. One day he realized, "I'm sexualizing my _____."

9. Discuss with your therapist any emotions or feelings that Kyle could be sexualizing. Consider these possible examples: obsessive curiosity, desire for adventure, itching for fun, need to feel more adult.

_____

_____

_____

_____

_____

_____

10. Discuss with your therapist what the possible triggers might be for these examples.

_____

_____

_____

_____

_____

EXAMPLE FOUR - Ben

When Ben was little, a teenage boy raped him. It happened several times. It was painful and left him embarrassed and ashamed. He found himself afraid of the teen and avoided him whenever possible. On a separate occasion, Ben was playing cops and robbers with some kids down the street. He was a robber. When they caught him, they tied his hands and punched him in the gut. It was going too far and soon they had taken his clothes off and kicked him between the legs. He laid on the ground embarrassed and ashamed. He was humiliated and never told anyone. The memory of what happened stuck in his head. He wanted to cut himself or hurt himself to make the images go away. Eventually this started showing up in his sexual feelings. He had thoughts about doing sexual things that involved pain. Sometimes he would fantasize about having others do sexual things to him that would be humiliating - like tying him up and calling him names while doing something sexual.

11. One day he realized, "I'm sexualizing my _____."

12. Discuss with your therapist any emotions or feelings that Ben could be sexualizing. Consider these possible examples: trauma of the abuse, need to feel safe, desire to resolve the hurt.

_____

_____

_____

_____

_____

_____

13. Discuss with your therapist what the possible triggers might be for these examples.

_____

_____

_____

_____

EXAMPLE FIVE - Tait

Tait was an athletic teenager who loved to play sports. He was popular and had many friends, but Tait never felt close to anyone. He longed to feel as though someone would let him into their private personal world. Most of his friends were superficial and didn't talk about personal things. He longed for deeper friendships. He wanted a girl he could talk to about his feelings - someone who would share her feelings with him and be real. He tried to socialize, but no one let him in and his relationships all felt superficial. Eventually this starting showing up in his sexual feelings. He started to watch girls coming in and out of the locker room, hoping to see them undressed. He fantasized about going by a girl's house after dark to peek in her window, hoping to see her undress. He even started walking by the changing areas in the store to see if he could glimpse a peek at someone when the door opened.

14. One day he realized, "I'm sexualizing my _____."

15. Discuss with your therapist any emotions or feelings that Tait could be sexualizing. Consider these possible examples: need for social connection, need to be open and real with someone, desire to be emotionally close to someone.

_____

_____

_____

_____

_____

_____

16. Discuss with your therapist what the possible triggers might be for these examples.

_____

_____

_____

_____

_____

EXAMPLE SIX - Aaron

Aaron grew up disconnected from his father who worked obsessively. Aaron's girlfriend was very supportive and helped him feel connection, but he didn't seem to have any adult men in his life that sincerely cared about him. He found himself jealous when the basketball coach spent extra time with other boys on the team. He day-dreamed about having a father who cared about him. Sometimes he stayed after school to ask a male teacher for tutoring, simply to get more attention from a mentor. When the teacher placed his hand on Aaron's shoulder to encourage him, he almost cried. Eventually this starting showing up in his sexual feelings, and he started looking at pornography that involved older men.

17. One day he realized, "I'm sexualizing my _____."

18. Discuss with your therapist any emotions or feelings that Aaron could be sexualizing. Consider these possible examples: father-hunger, desire for mentoring, need for guidance, sense of value.

_____

_____

_____

_____

_____

_____

19. Discuss with your therapist what the possible triggers might be for these examples.

_____

_____

_____

_____

_____

_____

EXAMPLE SEVEN - Ryder

Ryder grew up with a house full of sisters. Everything seemed to revolve around the girls in his house - dance lessons, dresses, sewing, theatre, make-up, and other activities in which his sisters engaged . Ryder's mother was constantly preoccupied with his sisters. She didn't have much time for him. He was hungry for her attention. Sometimes he imagined her giving him attention like tucking him in at night. One day when he was alone at home and a bit depressed. He went into his mother's room. He looked through her dresses and pressed the beautiful clothing against his cheeks. It was soft and comforting. It smelled like his mom. He found himself excited by the comfort. He repeated this experience many times as he grew into a teenager. Eventually this starting showing up in his sexual feelings. He started using his mother's clothes when he masturbated. Sometimes he would secretly take his sisters clothing and fantasize while looking at pornography. Once he even tried on his sister's underwear to get aroused.

20. One day he realized, "I'm sexualizing my _____."

21. Discuss with your therapist other needs Ryder could he be sexualizing. Consider these possible examples: mother-hunger, desire for feminine attention, longing for affection.

_____

_____

_____

_____

22. Discuss with your therapist what the possible triggers might be for these examples.

_____

_____

_____

_____

WHAT'S NEXT?

Included at the end of this workbook are pages which you can use as a **journal** to write down any thoughts or questions that you think of. You might want to address issues from your journal with your personal therapist. Additionally you can record your successes in the **sobriety tracker** at the end of this workbook.

When you have completed all of the tasks for the rank of Warrior in the Band of Brothers Program your therapist will date and sign your **Certificate of Completion** found at the end of this workbook.

MY JOURNAL

MY JOURNAL

_____
_____
_____
_____
_____
_____
_____
_____
_____
_____
_____
_____
_____
_____
_____
_____
_____
_____
_____
_____
_____
_____
_____
_____
_____
_____
_____
_____
_____

MY JOURNAL

MY JOURNAL

_____

_____

_____

_____

_____

_____

_____

_____

_____

_____

_____

_____

_____

_____

_____

_____

_____

_____

_____

_____

_____

_____

_____

_____

_____

_____

_____

_____

_____

MY JOURNAL

MY JOURNAL

MY JOURNAL

MY JOURNAL

_____
_____
_____
_____
_____
_____
_____
_____
_____
_____
_____
_____
_____
_____
_____
_____
_____
_____
_____
_____
_____
_____
_____
_____
_____
_____
_____
_____
_____

SOBRIETY TRACKER

MONTH:

SUNDAY	MONDAY	TUESDAY	WEDNESDAY	THURSDAY	FRIDAY	SATURDAY

MONTH:

SUNDAY	MONDAY	TUESDAY	WEDNESDAY	THURSDAY	FRIDAY	SATURDAY

MONTH:

SUNDAY	MONDAY	TUESDAY	WEDNESDAY	THURSDAY	FRIDAY	SATURDAY

MONTH:

SUNDAY	MONDAY	TUESDAY	WEDNESDAY	THURSDAY	FRIDAY	SATURDAY

SOBRIETY TRACKER

MONTH:

SUNDAY	MONDAY	TUESDAY	WEDNESDAY	THURSDAY	FRIDAY	SATURDAY

MONTH:

SUNDAY	MONDAY	TUESDAY	WEDNESDAY	THURSDAY	FRIDAY	SATURDAY

MONTH:

SUNDAY	MONDAY	TUESDAY	WEDNESDAY	THURSDAY	FRIDAY	SATURDAY

MONTH:

SUNDAY	MONDAY	TUESDAY	WEDNESDAY	THURSDAY	FRIDAY	SATURDAY

SOBRIETY TRACKER

MONTH:

SUNDAY	MONDAY	TUESDAY	WEDNESDAY	THURSDAY	FRIDAY	SATURDAY

MONTH:

SUNDAY	MONDAY	TUESDAY	WEDNESDAY	THURSDAY	FRIDAY	SATURDAY

MONTH:

SUNDAY	MONDAY	TUESDAY	WEDNESDAY	THURSDAY	FRIDAY	SATURDAY

MONTH:

SUNDAY	MONDAY	TUESDAY	WEDNESDAY	THURSDAY	FRIDAY	SATURDAY

CONGRATULATIONS WARRIOR!

Congratulations for completing Workbook 3! You have achieved Warrior rank and have earned your third certificate. The next step on your journey will be found in Workbook 4 where you'll be working toward the rank of Master Warrior.

Certificate of Completion

WARRIOR

Is Awarded To

_____

This individual has completed all of the tasks for the rank of Warrior in the Band of Brothers Program.

_____
Date

_____
Therapist

GUIDE BOOKS

The Arsenal

Mentor's Guide

Parent's Guide

WORKBOOKS

Workbook 1: Guardian

Workbook 2: Master Guardian

Workbook 3: Warrior

Workbook 4: Master Warrior

Workbook 5: Commander